THE GOOSE AND THE KANGAROO
(oo as in cool)

Mr. Goose sat near the cool
blue water playing the flute.

One day, Mr. Kangaroo came to him and said, "Mr. Goose, this June I am moving to the moon on my balloon. Very soon, I will build an igloo there and live in it."

"Don't be a fool! Do you know the balloon can't take you to the moon? Come, sit down. Pick up a spoon and eat some food. Think over what I said," said Mr. Goose.

Soon, they saw Mr. Baboon
passing by. He was wearing
high boots and carried a flute.

'Where are you going, Mr. Baboon? asked
Mr. Goose.
"Oh! I have a photo shoot. Very soon, I will
be a famous baboon," replied Mr. Baboon.

Mr. Kangaroo forgot all about the moon and asked Mr. Baboon if he could also go with him for the photo shoot. He added, "I'm sure 'photo' would be very tasty to eat fresh after the shoot."

Mr. Kangaroo, as you guess by now, was a foolish creature.

Mike is a five-year old child who loves to ride
his white, new bike.

Spite is a nine-year old who is not at all polite.

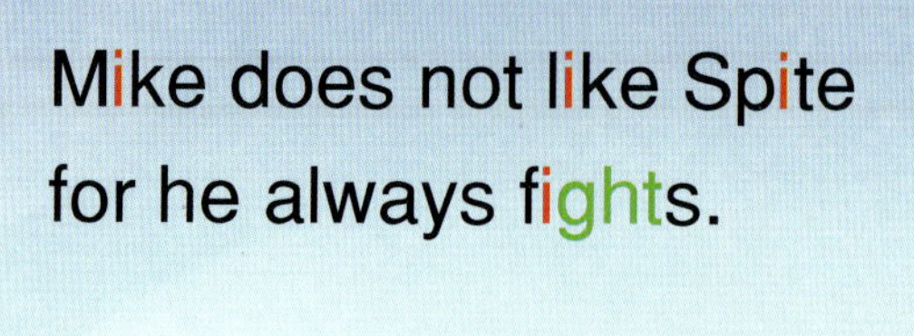

Mike does not like Spite
for he always fights.

One night, while Mike was eating
his favourite lime ice cream,
Spite gave him a real fright.

He disguised himself as a
crocodile and came whining
and sliding towards Mike.

Mike dropped his ice cream and prepared for a flight. When Spite removed his disguise, Mike cried, "This is not right!"

"Don't mind, it was a joke! Alright!" said Spite.
"Come on, give me a bright smile.
A wide smile did brighten the frightened Mike's
face. The two became friends and Spite was
no longer impolite.

DOREEN, THE STREET GIRL
(ee as in bee)

Doreen is a nineteen-year old girl who sweeps the streets.

Every night, she would creep between the trees to steal some sleep.

One night, when Doreen was in deep sleep, she had a dream that she was a queen.

Doreen, the Queen, sat on a large green leaf which
floated along with the breeze down a stream.
A huge Bumblebee was there to greet the Queen.

She was being served cheese, toffees and peaches with tea made rich with cream.

She had heaps of things to eat!

Just then, someone screamed and
Doreen's sweet dream was shattered.
That was the sad end of such a wonderful
dream of Doreen, the street girl.

ROSA AND THE WIZARD
(i as in bird and schwa as in ago)

Rosa lived with her mother near a river. Birds chirped gaily and butterflies flitted all over.

Rosa wished that all animals became her friends so that she could play with them forever.

Once, a good wizard granted her wish. Rosa heard a soft purring sound. She became alert and looked all around, for a kitten.

She was surprised to see a tiger, a
leopard and a panther. At first, she did not stir
but when she saw that the animals were not
stern, she mustered all her courage and patted
them without any fear.

Just then, an alligator on a surfboard and in
a bodysuit zipped up the river.

Rosa sat wondering whether she was dreaming when she heard, "Rosa wake up or you'll miss the bus and your teacher will be upset."
Why do such lovely things happen only in a dream, Rosa wondered!!

MISS **GRUNDY'S** **GR**EAT DANE
(**gr** as in **grand**)

Miss Grundy was a grand Greek lady. She loved to eat grapes and pomegranates.

She had a Great Dane for a pet and was very fond of him. She called him Graham.

Every day, the Great Dane, Graham woke Miss Grundy up with an angry growl for he was always hungry and greedy. Graham had a great appetite. He wanted bread made of black gram ground well with plenty of grated cheese added to it.

3

An old cook with grey hair agreed to grill it for Miss Grundy's Great Dane, Graham every morning.

Graham greeted the cook with great joy for the cook fed him and took him for a walk in the ground covered with green grass.

Graham would no longer
be a grumpy dog for
this was a great treat for
Graham, Miss Grundy's
Great Dane.

FRANKIE MONKEY'S FRIENDSHIP
(nk as in Frank)

Frankie Monkey lived on a tree on the bank of a river. He was always upto some prank or the other. All animals were tired of his pranks.

Juan the Donkey who lived nearby avoided Frankie Monkey. Juan the Donkey wore a tiny bell around his neck which tinkled whenever he moved.

One day he went to the lake in a cranky mood. He wanted to drink some water but he slipped and began to sink. Juan, the Donkey's mind went blank with fear.

Frankie Monkey,in a wink of an eye, climbed down the tree trunk and saved the sinking Juan the donkey.

Juan the Donkey thanked Frankie Monkey. Then the two friends had a drink made with some honey.

Juan the Donkey forgave Frankie for all his pranks and both thanked God for giving them such a good friend.

FIONA BUTTERFLY (**fl** as in **fly**)

Fiona Butter**fl**y loves to **fl**it from one **fl**ower to the other.

One day, a flamingo, the colour of a flame was flying high in the sky. Just then, he flipped, floated in air and within no time, fell on the floor. The flamingo had been hit with a flint by a heartless hunter.

A flock of sheep with pure white fleece saw the flamingo fall but did nothing. Fiona Butterfly and Flora Housefly saw how the sheep had behaved.

They picked up a flask of medicine, rushed to the flamingo and poured the medicine on the flamingo's flesh.

The flaming red flamingo was cured. She thanked
Fiona Butterfly and Flora Housefly for their help.

She promised to remain their friend and flew back to her nest where her baby flamingos waited for her.

SINATRA (**tr** as in **trap**)

This is a **tr**ue story about a wai**tr**ess who s**tr**uggled hard and became an ac**tr**ess. She was indeed very a**tr**active. Her name was Sina**tr**a.

One day, she sat near a tree trunk. She was trying to play the trumpet.

Just then far in the trackless field she saw something like a huge straw hat, land. Sinatra was too dazed by what she saw. Just then the object which looked like a straw hat changed its shape and looked like a huge flat tray. An astronaut came out of it. He was on a small tricycle. He came to Sinatra and said, "My name is Trink. Will you travel with me to space, my treasure?"

Sinatra thought that it might be a trap. How can I trust a stranger? The astronaut could read her mind and said, "No, it is not a trap. Believe me, pretty young lady. After the trip in space I will bring you back right here.

Sinatra really wished to travel in space. So she went with the astronaut, Trink.

23

Trink kept his promise. Now, whenever, Sinatra wishes to travel in space, she thinks of Trink. Within seconds, he is there, ready to take Sinatra for a trip in space.

BILL AND THE FISH
(i as in sit and ll as in fill)

"Bill see, there's a pink
fish in the pit," cried Jill.

"Is it ill? Will you pick
it up, Bill? said Jill.

"I will fill a bit of water in this tin dish
and dip the fish in it", said Jill.
"Grip it well or it will slip, Bill.

4

It spins and flicks its fin.

Now it seems
fit to do a Jig!!

OLD MONDY MOLE
(o as in hole)

Mondy Mole walked along the road which was covered
with snow.
He was pushing his wheelbarrow
full of toads to be sold.

He was growing old and so felt very cold.
He wore a coat and over it, an overcoat,
yet his throat was hoarse due to cold.

As he reached the shore, he
saw the steamboat float away.
Low in spirit, Mondy Mole sat
down near a pole. His toes hurt.

Just then, Jolly Goat rode by on her favourite Joan, the Foal.

She said to Mondy Mole, "Grandpa, don't lose hope. We will race along the shore and catch the steamboat at the port.

Mondy Mole rose. His spirit soared and off he went with the dear Jolly Goat.

BRAVE HEART MARCUS
(a as in arm and rk as in park)

Mark is a retired army man.
He now lives on a farm.
He starts his task very early
in the morning

His son, Marcus loves to bask on the
calm beach with lots of palm trees.

He hunts sharks
with darts and a
harpoon.

Once, a shark charged at him
but Marcus was not alarmed.
He has a big scar on his arm
but Marcus is a brave heart.

Marcus is now a famous artist who paints on
the barks of trees in the park, near the market.

He is also a pop star who sings
and plays the guitar and the harp.
Marcus has won everyone's hearts.

MR. CRUNCH THE BUFFALO
(ch as in church and u as in bun)

Mr. Crunch the Buffalo waited for the bus with a bundle of grass to munch. He was very cheerful for he was going to meet his chum, Mr. Dumb, the Buck, for lunch.

What fun I will have with my childhood
buddy—humming in the sun and playing
the drums, thought Mr. Crunch.

Just then, Mr. Jump, the
Bug and Miss Cherrie, the
Bumblebee whizzed past him
and bumped into a branch.

All the chestnuts which Mr. Jump
carried fell into the mud.
"How clumsy you are!" cried
Miss Cherrie, the Bumblebee.

Mr. Jump, the Bug blushed and looked
very glum. He mumbled," Miss Cherrie,
I am sorry. It was a blunder."

"Oh, don't worry, dear Miss Cherrie. I have a cheese and honey sandwich which both of us will eat, sitting on the rug with a mug of chilled chocolate shake.

Freddie was a frisky little frog. She loved to wear frilly frocks. She always sat on a toadstool which she called Freddie Frog's throne.

Freddie sat all day long eating French fries.

Mummy Frog frowned and fretted to see Freddie Frog turn fat from fit.

"Wake up early and go for a walk in the fresh morning air when the fruits are covered with frost,"said Mummy Frog.

Daddy Frog added,"Yes! That will also free you from freckles.Otherwise, one day you will become a freak and all the other frogs will be frightened of you.

Freddie Frog listened to her parents' advice and she is back to being a frisky and fit frog.

TRAMP SCAMP (**mp** as in **stamp**)

One day, old Tra**mp** Sca**mp** sat cra**mp**ed in a da**mp** corner.

Just then, Grumpy who was an umpire in the cricket team and who looked like a vampire dumped a heap of trash. All of it fell on Tramp Scamp's head.

Poor Tramp Scamp got a large bump on his head. "This is not the way to treat simple people," said the grumpy Tramp Scamp.

Tramp Scamp started searching the trash and found a rare stamp. He also found an old lamp.

Tramp Scamp rubbed the lamp to clean it. Suddenly an impressive genie stood before him, saying, "What can I do for you my lord?"

"Make me the emperor of this land. There should not be a single miserable tramp in this huge empire .They will all have bread to eat and a house to live but before you do that rid me of my smelly damp rags.

The very next moment, Tramp Scamp disappeared and in his place stood a handsome emperor. He did what he promised and in that empire there are no poor tramps any longer.

STELLA THE STAR (st as in story)

You must read this strange and interesting story.
One day, while on a stroll, Stella stepped into a puddle
of stale rain water. A stone got stuck to her shoe.

Stella took a stick and tried to remove it. Still it stayed stuck to her shoe.

Stella was a strong girl. She kicked the stone hard.

Then a strange thing happened. The stone started to sparkle like a star. It flitted around Stella casting a bright light on her.

16

The very next moment, it shot past Stella
up in the sky. It happened so fast that
Stella simply stood and stared.

Now the stone has become a bright and
sparkling star known as Stella Star.

BEN PENGUIN
(ng as in ring)

"Hurry! Ring the gong. My friend, Ben Penguin is in trouble. I saw a single stranger hanging around in the jungle," said Kangaroo Kong to the king of the Jungle Mungle.

The king was very angry.

He engaged some rangers and ordered, "Bring the stranger to me.

We will ha**ng** him. My animals must be free to mi**ng**le with others without any da**ng**er.

Just then, they heard a ba**ng** and the ga**ng** of ra**ng**ers saw the stra**ng**er da**ng**le from a branch of the ma**ng**o tree.

Ben Penguin congratulated the King and began to sing praises of his friend, Kangaroo Kong and the King of Jungle Mungle.

PAT, JACK'S FAT CAT
(**a** as in **cat** and **sh** as in **ship**)

Pat is Jack's fat cat.

He is shy and lazy.

He sits on a mat in the

shade and naps.

One day, Pat saw a rat. It ran
down the shelf and hid under
a shawl kept near a hat.

Jack's Dad, in his shorts and jacket, sat eating a sandwich and fishing, near his shack, on the beach.

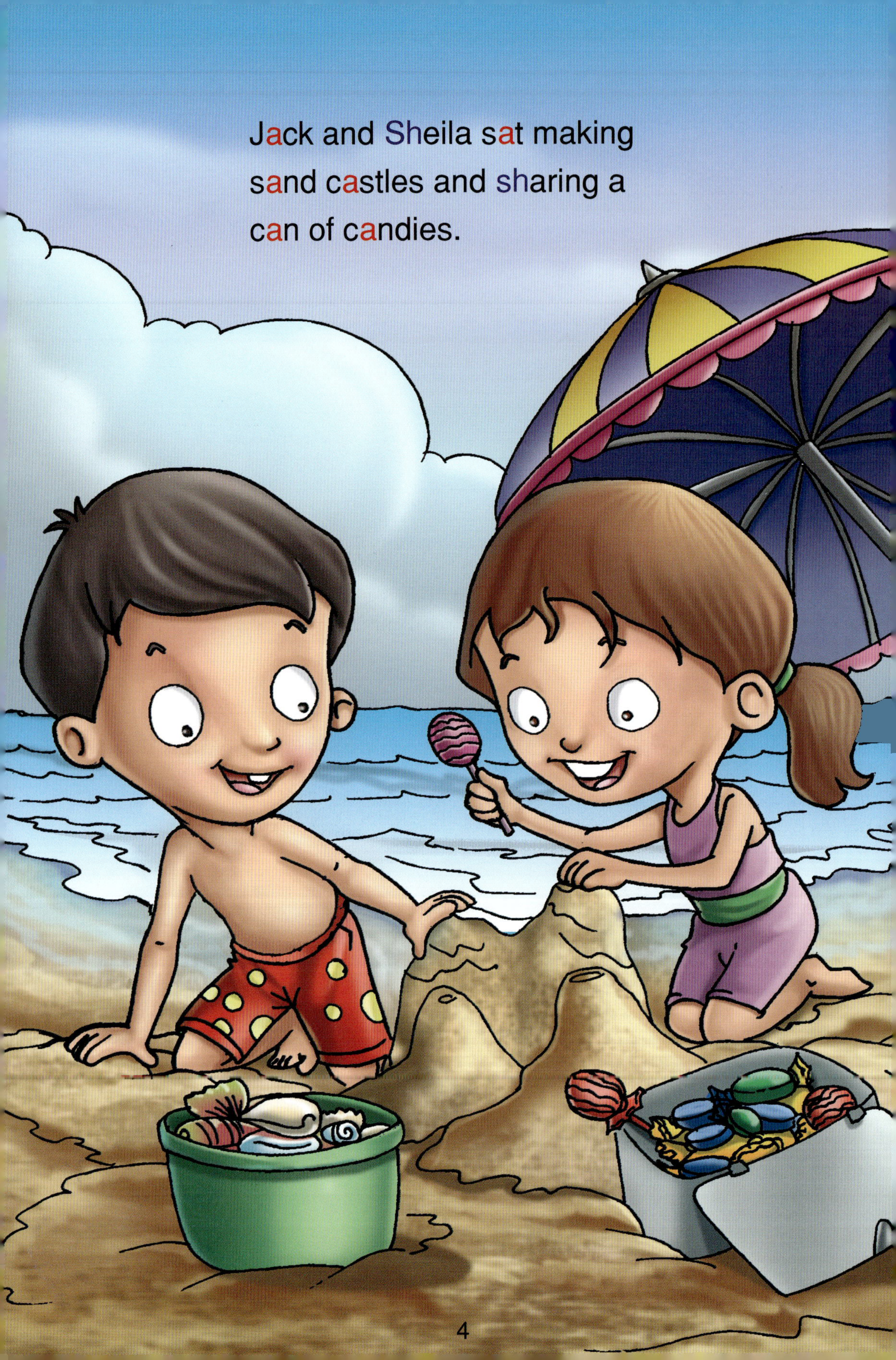
Jack and Sheila sat making
sand castles and sharing a
can of candies.

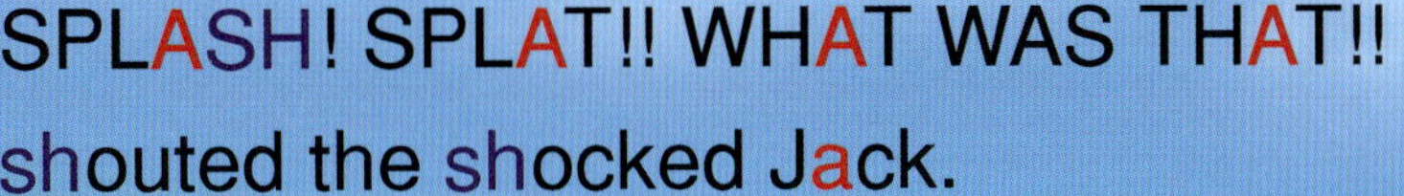

SPLASH! SPLAT!! WHAT WAS THAT!!
shouted the shocked Jack.

Mad Pat, Jack's fat cat, dashed to catch the rat and landed in a shallow pan on the gas. That was the sad end of Pat, the cat who tried to catch a rat.

BETTY AND DELLA
(e as in pet and th as in them)

Mummy, let me check who rang the bell.
I bet it is my pet hen, Betty. Can you guess?

She is all set on Jenny Elephant's head.How did she get there? Oops!

Betty fell from Jenny Elephant's
head. Her feathers are all wet.
Look! Her dress is in such a mess!

"Mummy shall I take Betty to the vet?"

Della dear, first eat the egg which I shelled and put on the slice of bread. Then eat your ice cream before it melts.

Take your Teddy along. Look!
He's all set to go to bed. I bet
the weather will clear his head.
That will help them both Betty
and the Teddy.

TOM'S JOG
(o as in pot)

Tom is a cop. He lives in a house
made of logs. He loves Bob, his dog.

One day, he went for a jog along the bog, with his dog, Bob.

He was shocked to see John, the Swan
in a polka dot frock, eating hot dogs.

Jolly, the Fox sat nearby
with a box of popcorn.

Lotto, the Frog hopped about
and then sat on top of a rock
with a wasp on his fishing rod.

Tom the cop could not believe his eyes.
Even Bob, his dog forgot to bark.
Now, every morning, Tom goes for a jog
along the bog.

APE JANE'S BIRTHDAY
(ei as in day)

Jane and Jake are baby apes. Everyday, their maid made them wash their faces which they hated.

"Why do you make us do that? Tell us why don't we have a tail to shake the dirt away?" they complained.

Jake was very lazy. He lay in the shade all day and ate grapes but Jane liked to play. "Play with me Jake," she would say but lazy Jake did not obey.

Just then, she saw Drake,
Snake and Snail pass by
their gate.

"Hey, come in! Have you forgotten the date? Today is my birthday. Let's celebrate," said Jane.

The maid got the cake on a tray
which they all ate along with
strawberry shake, with great taste.

They played till eight and then went to the fete. Afterwards, they went to the lake where they sailed and sailed till late.

Alex Alligator ate apples and apricots in the afternoon.

Ben, the Baboon, bought a big bicycle on his brother's birthday.

Carol Caterpillar cut a cake and crawled on the carpet to watch a cartoon clip.

D

Dainty Diana, Daddy's darling daughter loves delicious doughnuts.

Elma Egret got into the elevator to see an eagle sitting on an elephant, eating an egg.

Fat Freddie Frog fell on the floor.

Gracie Goat got a
great gift from her granny.

H

Harry Horse has a
huge hare on his hat.

Ila's pet Incy Iguana loves ice cream
who loves ice cream.

Jack, the Jaguar and Jill,
the Jackal live in the jungle.

K

Katy
Kangaroo
loves to fly
kites.

L

Linda Lioness
loves lettuce,
lamb chops
and lollipops.

M

Maria Monkey's mommy made
a magic mat for her moppet.

Nelly Nightingale never returns
to her nest before noon.

Olof Ocelot ate an orange and an omelette and was off to meet Olive Octopus.

Pamela Pigeon put her pen and pencil
in the pink pouch and left for the party.

Queeny Quail has a
quilt which keeps her
quite warm.

R
Ronnie Rabbit
ran a race with
Rocky the Ram.

S

Spider Sam sat
sipping strawberry
juice on a sunny,
Sunday morning.

T

Tiger Tim took
Tambie the
Tortoise and
Taira the teal
for a trek.

U

Umer's Uncle has an ugly Unicorn
under his umbrella.

V

Victor Vulture loves to eat
vegetables and play the violin.

Walter Walrus wore a white waistcoat and went to work.

Alex fixed a xylophone, put it in a box and gave it as a
gift to Max on Xmas.

Yasmine has a yak which eats yam.
It sits near Yasmine's yellow yacht and
yawns all the year round.

Y

Zara Zebra zipped to Zaire to see a chimpanzee and a lizard. Wasn't that crazy?

JOLLY BROTHERS: JACOB AND ROGER
(j as in Jacob)

Jacob loved jam and jelly. His younger brother, Roger wanted jujubes all the time.

Their Mummy was angry, "No more jam, jelly or jujubes for both of you! You must eat lots of vegetables and drink juice."

"Just once, please fill the jars! Requested Jacob and Roger.

"No! Remember vegetables and fruit juice, first. Then I will think about your request," replied their mother.

Jacob and Roger were sad. Is there no magic that will give me lots of jujubes?" said Roger—"and fill all the jars with jam and jelly!" added Jacob.

Just then a generous and gentle fairy appeared before them and said, "I heard you both. I can grant your wish on one condition.
Promise to eat vegetables and have lots of juice.
Then your jars will have plenty of jam, jelly and jujubes.

Jacob and Roger agreed. The fairy waved her wand and the next moment there was a jug of juice and a basket of fruits before them on the table. As the two boys bit into an apple and had some juice, the jars were filled with jam, jelly and jujubes as the fairy promised.

Now they are very happy and healthy.
Mummy is also happy for her sons
have started eating healthy food.

FYODOR AND THE DINOSAUR
(oo as in door)

I will tell you a story about Fyodor. He loved to play indoors. He sat on the floor and made sketches on a white board.

One morning, someone knocked. Before Fyodor could open the door, he saw huge claws in giant paws. The door was pushed open and a baby dinosaur crawled in.

Fyodor couldn't believe what he saw. The dinosaur wore a floral print frock .She told Fyodor that her name was Gorgie.

Gorgie told Fyodor that she wanted to play but had no friends. Fyodor lost all fear of the dinosaur and began to adore her.

Gorgie Dinosaur roared with delight and put Fyodor on her back.

The two had ice cream at a store at the shore and then had more fun, watching the waves soar.

THELMA THRUSH AND HER FRIENDS
(th as in think)

Thelma Thrush, Theodore Python and Dotty Moth are thick friends. One would think it impossible but the three friends were bound by a strong thread of friendship.

It was Dotty Mo**th**'s bir**th**day. **Th**eodore Py**th**on made a
thick bro**th** which was full of fro**th**.
Thelma **Thr**ush **th**rew in some **th**yme.

The three friends were very thrilled
playing with each other.

Thelma Thrush said, " Don't you think we should sleep for a while?" Dotty Moth threw a thin pillow at her and shouted, "No! My birthday comes only once a year. Do you think we should waste it by sleeping?"

The three friends enjoyed themselves through the
night.

In the morning, they thanked Dotty Moth and returned
home.

FLOYD AND TROY
(oi as in boy and nt as in pint)

Floyd was a royal boy. He hated to toil. Troy was his loyal servant. Floyd loved to play with his servant boy, Troy.

All day, Floyd spent his time playing with his toys and was full of joy.

20

One day he got a boil. He asked Troy to put some ointment on his boil.

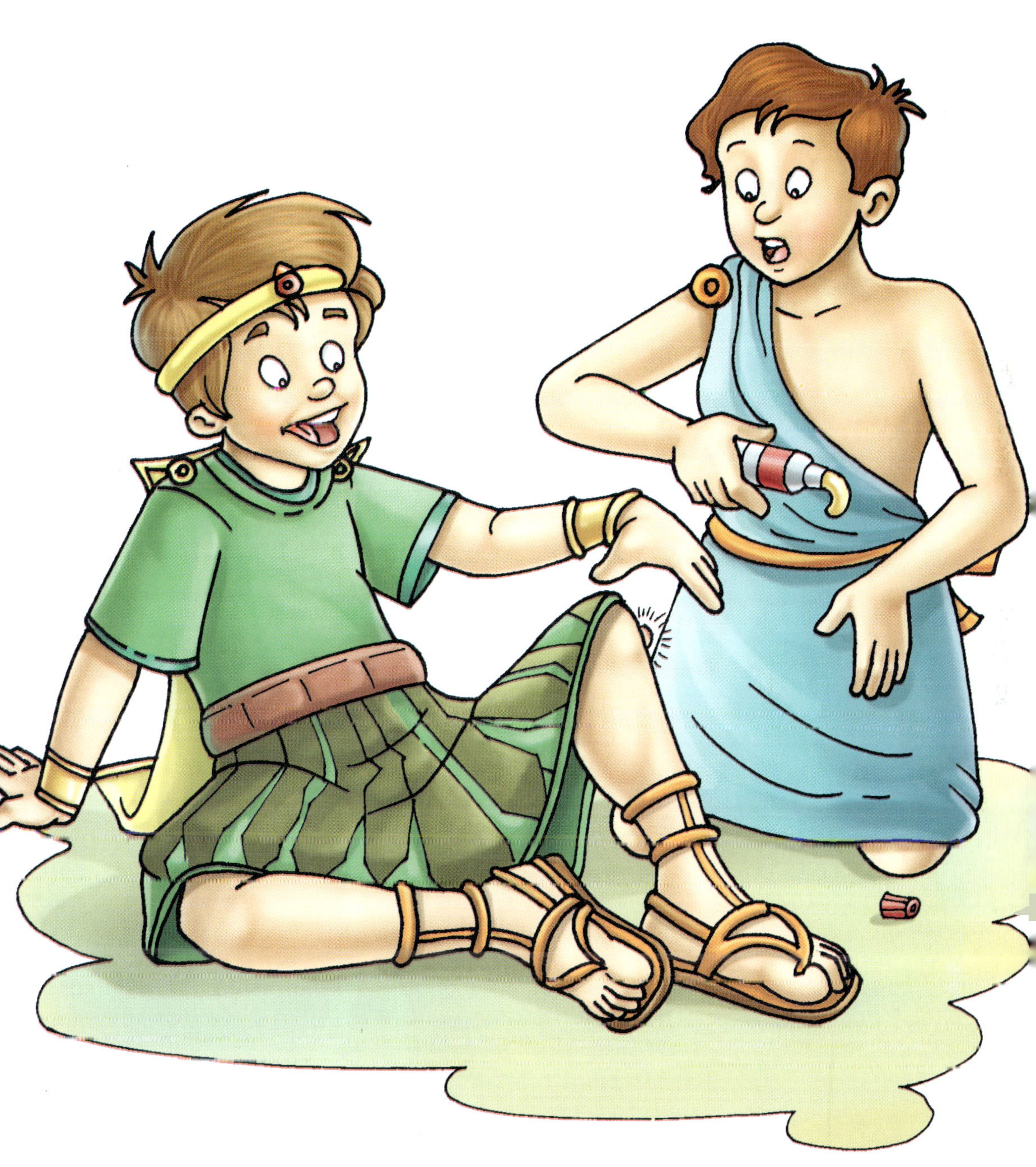

Troy put the ointment on the boil and also gave Floyd a pint of oyster oil.

"I hate it! It is like poison! Throw it on the soil and don't go beyond that point. You can't disturb me. Come and join me, let's play this interesting game: Coin and the tinted foil.

Troy went and joined Floyd the royal boy, as he had no choice.

BEAR CLARE'S PEAR

(air as in pear and nd as in ground)

Bear Clare sat on a rocking chair, enjoying the cool air and eating a pear.

"How d**are** you!" boomed a voice.
What was that sou**nd**, thought B**ear** Cl**are** to himself. He was sc**are**d and he looked arou**nd**.
Then he st**are**d in one spot and saw Gren**d**a M**are**. "It's unf**air**! That was my p**ear**! grumbled Gren**d**a M**are**.

Just then, Sandy Hare came running down
the stairs in top gear.

Grenda Marc and Clare Bear forgot all about the pear.
"Where are you coming from in such a hurry? Did you
not repair the chair?" asked Bear Clare.
"Listen friends, we will not go to the fair," said Sandy
Hare.

Bear Clare and Grenda Mare glared at Sandy Hare and said, "Why should we miss the fair?"
"A snare has been set up there. I care for my friends so I shared the news," said Sandy Hare.

So the friends believed Sandy Hare and decided not to go to the fair. Instead, they played there and after saying their prayers, the three went to bed.

LUKE THE DUKE (u as in cube)

Luke was a duke who grew tired of his duty and the boring schedule.

Luke decided to do something new. He drew up a plan to sail to an island which was famous for its sand dunes.

The crew blew the bugle and off they set sail in the blue waters.
The captain in his uniform threw the anchor on reaching the island.

'Why have we stopped? Have we run out of fuel?"
asked Luke, who was busy solving the Rubik Cube.

"Don't fret and f**u**me, Luke. Look around. The island is full of beauty. See so many t**u**na fish! They are so h**u**ge!" exclaimed the Captain.

Yes Captain, you are right. The island is full of beauty, though it is very humid. Let's hear some music. That's a lovely tune! Look at those tulips in such a variety of hues!" exclaimed Luke happily.

The gruelling journey had been truly rewarding. After a week's stay on the island, Luke was ready to get back to his duty.

THE CLOWN MR. BROWN
(ow as in how)

Mr. Brown is a clown but you will never see him without a scowl. He is always in a foul mood.

His friend, Mr. Owl wears a crown and loudly plays the mouth organ to make his friend, Mr. Brown laugh.

Moo-Moo, the Cow is also their friend. She jokes around wearing a brown gown roaming all over the town.

Mr. Mouse, their friend, jumps up and down trying to put groundnuts in Mr. Brown's mouth.

Finally, they succeed in removing the frown from Mr. Brown's face. Mr. Brown is now truly a clown.

Happily, they live in a house down
south surrounded by lots of clouds.

THE DEER AND THE TERRIER
(ee as in dear)

Mr. Deer had never seen a terrier.
So, one day when he saw one,
he was full of fear.

Mrs. Deer asked, "What happened, dear?
Why have you put these barriers here?"

Mr. Deer replied, "It was essential. Do you hear that sound? It is echoing in my ears. Promise me, you will keep it confidential."

"Yes, my dear. Tell me clearly and fearlessly. What is the matter?"

Mr. Deer told his wife that a strange animal fills him with fear.

"Don't you worry, husband dear. That animal is merely a terrier. I will smear this on your face.

Soon you will have a thick b**ea**rd. Then you will no longer f**ea**r the terr**ie**r. In fact, the terr**ie**r will f**ea**r you. Now ch**ee**r up, hubby d**ea**r.